Starter

LET'S GO

Student Book

by
R. Nakata
K. Frazier

with
songs and chants by Carolyn Graham

OXFORD
UNIVERSITY PRESS

OXFORD
UNIVERSITY PRESS

198 Madison Avenue,
New York, NY 10016 USA

Great Clarendon Street,
Oxford OX2 6DP England

Oxford New York
Auckland Bangkok Buenos Aires Cape Town Chennai
Dar es Salaam Delhi Hong Kong Istanbul Karachi Kolkata
Kuala Lumpur Madrid Melbourne Mexico City Mumbai Nairobi
São Paulo Shanghai Taipei Tokyo Toronto

OXFORD is a trademark of Oxford University Press.

ISBN 0-19-435290-0

Editorial Manager: Shelagh Speers
Editor: Lynne Robertson
Production Editor: Mark Steven Long
Elementary Design Manager: Doris Chen
Designer/Art Buyer: Bill Smith Studio
Production Manager: Abram Hall

Printing (last digit): 20 19 18 17 16 15 14

Printed in China.

Illustrations by George Ulrich
Block icons by Maj-Britt Hagsted

Cover design by April Okano, Brett Sonnenschein
Cover Illustration by Paul Meisel

Table of Contents

Lesson 1

ant

Alice

alligator

apple

5

Lesson 2

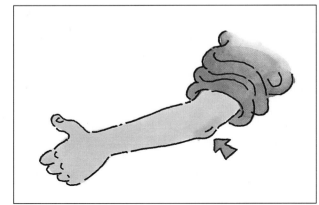

elbow

Eddie

egg

elephant

6

Lesson 3

ink

Isabel

igloo

insect

8

Lesson 4

octopus

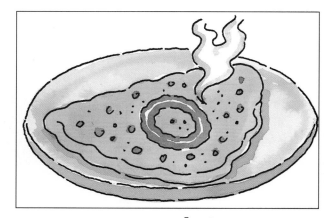

omelet

Oliver

ostrich

10

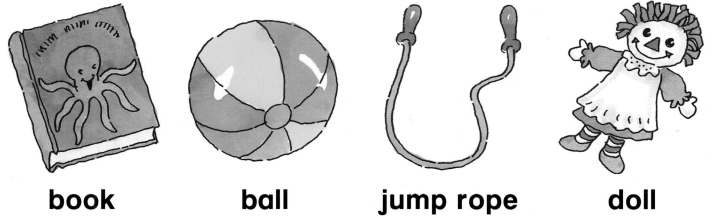

book   **ball**   **jump rope**   **doll**

Lesson 5

umpire

umbrella

Uncle Jim

upside-down

12

balloon

bicycle

top

net

Lesson 6

Beth

boy

bird

bag

1   one   2   two

3   three

4   four   5   five

Lesson 7

car

Carol

cat

candy

16

6   **six**

7   **seven**

8   **eight**

9   **nine**

10   **ten**

dog

desk

David

dinosaur

Lesson 9

girl

gorilla

Gail

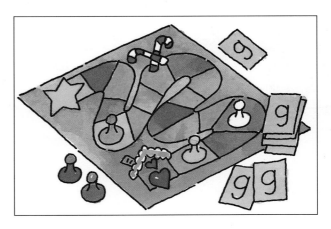

game

Lesson 10

peach

Peter

pencil

picture

22

pig

pigs

cow

cows

duck

ducks

Lesson 11

table

telephone

Tom

TV

24

taxi

taxis

truck

trucks

train

trains

Lesson 12

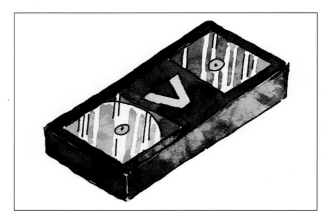

video

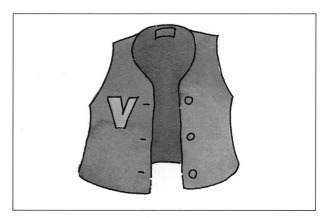

vest

Vicky

violin

26

27

Lesson 13

zebra

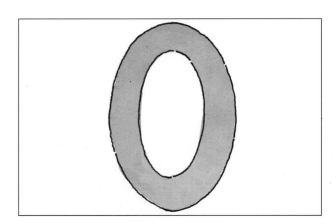

zero

Zack

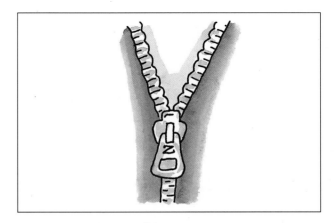

zipper

Lesson 14

finger

foot

Fay

fan

a circle   a square   a triangle   a rectangle

Lesson 15

lamb

Luke

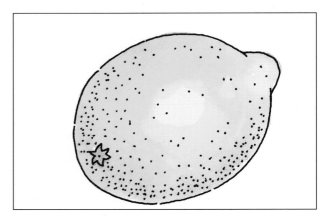

lemon

lion

a star   a diamond   a heart   an oval

Lesson 16

moon

Mary

man

monkey

34

Lesson 17

nut

notebook

Nina

nest

36

37

Lesson 18

sandwich

Sally

seesaw

sun

Lesson 19

X ray

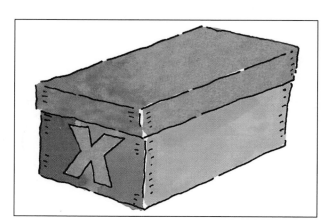

box

Mr. X

fox

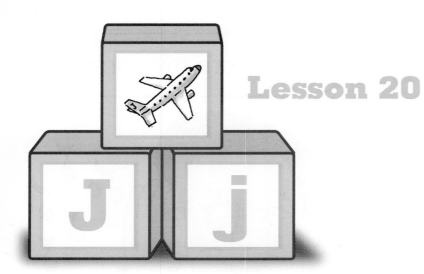

jam

juice

Jack

jet

43

Lesson 21

kitten

kite

Kim

kangaroo

44

45

Lesson 22

hat

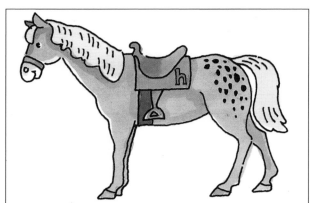

horse

Henry

house

47

Lesson 23

queen

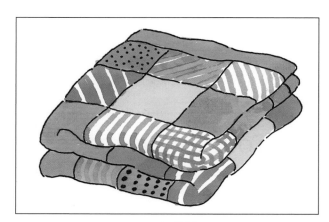

quilt

Quinn

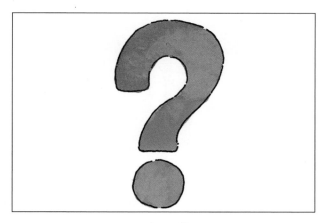

question

Lesson 24

rocket

Roger

rabbit

radio

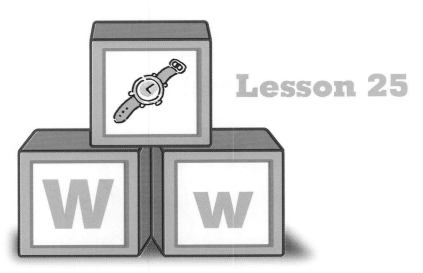

water

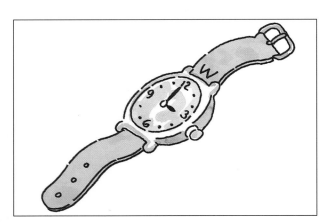

watch

Wendy

woman

yak

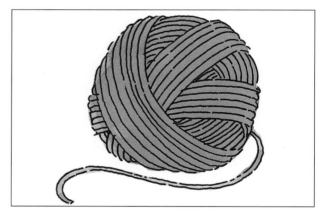

yarn

yo-yo

Yolanda

Lesson 27

A
B
C

H
I
J

N
O
P

56 T
U
V

Lesson 28

d
e
f
g

k
l
m

q
r
s

w
x
y
z

Let's Go Starter Syllabus

LESSON	LETTER	LANGUAGE ITEMS	FUNCTIONS	TOPICS
1	A a	Hi! Hello!	Greetings	Greetings
2	E e	What's your name? I'm (Sam).	Asking someone's name	Names
3	I i	Hi! How are you? I'm fine.	Greetings	Greetings
4	O o	What is it? It's a (book).	Identifying objects (singular)	Toys
5	U u	What is it? It's a (balloon).	Identifying objects (singular)	Toys
6	B b	Let's count! OK!	Counting 1–5	Numbers 1–5
7	C c	Let's count! OK!	Counting 6–10	Numbers 6–10
8	D d	How many? (7)!	Counting 1–10	Numbers 1–10
9	G g	How old are you? I'm (7).	Asking and telling age	Age
10	P p	What are they? They're (dogs).	Identifying objects (plural)	Animals
11	T t	What are they? They're (cars).	Identifying objects (plural)	Toys
12	V v	What color is it? It's (blue).	Identifying colors	Colors
13	Z z	What color is it? It's (pink).	Identifying colors	Colors
14	F f	What shape is it? It's (a circle).	Identifying shapes (with articles)	Shapes
15	L l	What shape is it? It's (a star).	Identifying shapes (with articles)	Shapes

LESSON	LETTER	LANGUAGE ITEMS	FUNCTIONS	TOPICS
16	M m	Good morning! Good night!	Greetings	Greetings
17	N n	Thank you! You're welcome.	Polite expressions	Polite expressions
18	S s	This is my (body).	Identifying parts of the body (singular)	Parts of the body
19	X x	These are my (eyes).	Identifying parts of the body (singular and plural)	Parts of the body
20	J j	These are my (arms).	Identifying parts of the body (plural)	Parts of the body
21	K k	This is my (left hand).	Identifying right and left	Right and left
22	H h	Touch your (shoulders).	Simple commands	Parts of the body
23	Q q	Ouch! I hurt my (knee)!	Expressing pain	Pain
24	R r	Let's go! (Up!) OK!	Simple commands	Direction
25	W w	I can (walk).	Expressing ability	Simple verbs
26	Y y	I can (swim).	Expressing ability	Simple verbs
27	A - Z	Capital letters A–Z	Alphabet	Alphabet
28	a - z	Small letters a–z	Alphabet	Alphabet
29	Good-bye	Good-bye! See you later!	Farewells	Farewells

Syllabus

Word List

A

a 4
a 11
A 4
alligator 4
an 33
ant 4
apple 4
are 9
arms 43

B

b 14
B 14
bag 14
ball 11
balloon 13
bicycle 13
bird 14
black 29
blue 27
body 39
book 11
box 40
boy 14
brown 29

C

c 16
C 16
can 53
candy 16
car 16
cat 16
circle 31
color 27
count 15
cow 23

D

d 18
D 18
dance 55
desk 18
diamond 33
dinosaur 18
dog 18
doll 11
down 51
duck 23

E

e 6
E 6
ears 41
egg 6
eight 17
elbow 6
elephant 6
eyes 41

F

f 30
F 30
face 39
fan 30
feet 43
fine 9
finger 30
five 15
foot 30
four 15
fox 40

G

g 20
G 20
game 20
girl 20
go 51
good morning 35
good night 35
good-bye 60
gorilla 20
green 27

H

h 46
H 46
hand 45
hat 46
head 39
heart 33
hello 5
hi 5
hop 55
horse 46
house 46
how 9
hurt 49

I

i 8
I 8
I 49
I'm 7
igloo 8
in 51
ink 8
insect 8
is 11
it 11
it's 11

J

j 42
J 42
jam 42
jet 42
juice 42
jump 53
jump rope 11

K

k 44
K 44
kangaroo 44
kite 44
kitten 44
knee 49

L

l 32
L 32
lamb 32
left 45
legs 43
lemon 32
let's 15
lion 32

M

m 34
M 34
man 34
many 19
monkey 34
moon 34
mouth 39
my 39

N

n 36
N 36
name 7
nest 36
net 13
nine 17
nose 41
notebook 36
nut 36

O

o 10
O 10
octopus 10
OK 15
old 21
omelet 10
one 15
orange 27
ostrich 10
ouch 49
out 51
oval 33

P

p 22
P 22
peach 22
pencil 22
picture 22
pig 23
pink 29
purple 29

Q

q 48
Q 48
queen 48
question 48
quilt 48

R

r 50
R 50
rabbit 50
radio 50
rectangle 31
red 27
right 45
rocket 50
run 53

S

s 38
S 38
sandwich 38
see you later 61
seesaw 38
seven 17
shape 31
shoulders 47
sing 55
six 17
skip 53
square 31
star 33
sun 38
swim 55

T

t 24
T 24
table 24
taxi 25
telephone 24
ten 17
thank you 37
these 41
they 23
they're 23
this 39
three 15
toes 47
top 13
touch 47
train 25
triangle 31
truck 25
turn around 51
TV 24
two 15

U

u 12
U 12
umbrella 12
umpire 12
uncle 12
up 51
upside-down 12

V

v 26
V 26
vest 26
video 26
violin 26

W

w 52
W 52
walk 53
watch 52
water 52
what 11
what's 7
white 29
woman 52

X

x 40
X 40
X ray 40

Y

y 54
Y 54
yak 54
yarn 54
yellow 27
yo-yo 54
you 9
you're welcome 37
your 7

Z

z 28
Z 28
zebra 28
zero 28
zipper 28